'T Pousette et 'T Poulette

'T Pousette et 'T Poulette

A Cajun Hansel and Gretel

Written by
Sheila Hebert-Collins

Illustrated by
Patrick Soper

PELICAN PUBLISHING COMPANY
Gretna 2001

This book is dedicated in memory of Regina Oubre Hollier, or
"Momee" to her grandchildren.
"Momee" had a favorite bedtime story she called
'T Pousette. Her story really influenced me.

This book is also dedicated to Angelica McMorris Cornett and
her eighth grade class of '98-'99 at French Settlement High School,
who helped me write this story. This was truly a
Cajun Team Effort we can be proud of.
Merci, to all those students, and please
continue to write with Cajun Pride!!

The word "Pelican" and the depiction of a pelican
are trademarks of Pelican Publishing Company, Inc., and are registered
in the US Patent and Trademark Office.

Library of Congress Cataloging-in-Publication Data

Collins, Sheila Hébert.
    'T Pousette et 't Poulette : a Cajun Hansel and Gretel / written by Sheila Hébert
Collins ; French editor, Barbara Hébert Hébert ; illustrated by Patrick Soper.
      p. cm.
    Summary: A Cajun version of the well-known tale in which two children are left in
the woods but find their way home despite an encounter with a wicked witch.
    ISBN 1-56554-764-0
    [1. Fairy tales. 2. Folklore—Germany.] I. Hébert, Barbara Hébert. II. Soper, Patrick,
ill. III. Hansel and Gretel. English. IV. Title.

PZ8.C6953 Ci 2001
[398.2]—dc21
[E]
                                                00-068461

Printed in Hong Kong

Published by Pelican Publishing Company, Inc.
1000 Burmaster Street, Gretna, Louisiana 70053

'T Pousette et 'T Poulette

Deep in the heart of the Louisiana swampland, there lived a poor fur trapper named *Vincent Seivicque*. His wife, Marie, had died of swamp fever, leaving him to care for his twins, *'T Pousette and 'T Poulette*. Times were hard for the *Seivicques* since the loggers had come to the swamp. Fewer trees meant fewer animals for the traps. Food was scarce in the *Seivicque* home.

Vincent Seivicque (veh son su vik) an Italian name "changed" to French by Grandpère Seivicque
'T Pousette (t poo set) Cajun nickname
'T Poulette (t poo let) Cajun nickname that means "little chicken"

One night the children were very restless because their little tummies were so empty. Papa tucked them into their beds and told them this story to settle them down: "This story is a legend around *La Côte Française*. Your *grandpère*, Nicholas Seivicque, was a *bon ami* to the pirate *Jean Lafitte*. It is said that one of *Lafitte's* ships sank near *Bayou Vincent*. On that ship was a great treasure. Legend says that an old alligator named *Cocodrie* lives in the swamp and guards *Lafitte's* treasure. Cocodrie even wears a tiara from the treasure as he swims along in the swamps. Now *mes petits enfants:* dream of *Lafitte's* treasure. "*Bonsoir, papa,*" said the children.

La Côte Francaise (lah coat fron sez) Original name for the French
  Settlement, Louisiana.
Nicholas (nick oh lah)
Grandpère (gron pair) Grandfather
bon ami (bon ah me) Good friend
Jean Lafitte (jzhon lu feet) French pirate
Cocodrie (co co dree) alligator
mes petits enfants (may pee tees on fon) my little children
bonsoir (bon swah) good night

With little money and food, the new stepmother, Lelia, was anxious to get rid of the children. One morning she tried to convince her husband to leave the children in the swamp. "Don't worry, *cher*, those loggers need some children to show them 'round the bayou. They will take good care of them."

cher (sha) darling

'T Pousette overheard Lelia, grabbed his coat, and ran out of the house. He walked along the bayou trying to think of a way to help. He grabbed a handful of broken oyster shells, filled his pockets, then went inside.

Later that day, Papa called out, *"'T Pousette and 'T Poulette, viens ici! It's time to bait the traps. Allons!"* 'T Pousette and 'T Poulette followed Papa and Lelia out into the swamp. As he walked along he dropped pieces of oyster shells. *"Dépêche toi!"* shouted Lelia to 'T Pousette. "I'm watching for *Cocodrie*," 'T Pousette responded. *"C'est fou!"* answered Lelia.

viens ici (vee yeh ee see) come here!
Allons! (ah lon) Let's go!

Dépêche toi! (de pesh twah) Hurry up!
C'est fou! (say foo) That's crazy!

When they had baited most of the traps, Papa stopped, built a fire, then said, "Stay here, *mes enfants*, while Lelia and I bait the rest of the traps." *'T Pousette* saw the sadness in Papa's eyes.

mes enfants (mayz on fon) my children

Night came but Papa did not return. *'T Poulette* started to cry. *"Pleure pas, 'T Poulette,"* comforted *'T Pousette.* "My oyster shells will lead us home." Sure enough, as the moon shone on the oyster shells, the children found their way home. Papa greeted them with big hugs. He was so ashamed. Lelia just shook her head.

Pleure pas (plur pah) Don't cry

The next day after Papa had left, Lelia called the children. "Let's take this *boudin* to Papa for lunch." *'T Pousette* didn't have time to get oyster shells so he just grabbed *le pain perdue* from the table and stuffed it into his pockets. As they walked through the swamp, *'T Pousette* lagged behind, dropping pieces of *le pain perdue* along the way. "*Depéche toi!* Before that *cocodrie* has you for lunch!" teased Lelia.

boudin (boo deh) cajun sausage
le pain perdue (ler peh per due) "lost" (stale) bread; French toast

After Papa had his lunch and left to bait more traps, Lelia built a fire and told the children to wait until she returned for them. Soon, the swamp was filled with darkness and the children started for home looking for their *pain perdue* trail. *Et La!* All *le pain perdue* was gone, eaten by the creatures in the swamp. *'T Poulette* started to cry.

Et la! (a lah) a cajun expression meaning "Of all things!"

"*Pleure pas, chere.*" said 'T Pousette. "Let's climb that tree and rest where the *cocodrie* won't find us." In the morning, the children started searching for berries, wandering deeper into the swamp. As they were about to faint from hunger, they heard the sound of *zydeco* music coming from yet deeper into the swamp. What a joy to their ears! Surely where there is good Cajun music, there will be *bonne cuisine.*

zydeco (zi du ko) fast, rhythmic Cajun music
bonne cuisine (bon kwee zeen) good cooking

They wasted no time following that *zydeco*. Suddenly, 'T Pousette stopped. "*Tu vois ca?*" he asked 'T Poulette. There in the distance stood a little cottage nestled under the cypress trees.

Tu vois ca? (too vwah sah) Do you see that?

As they came closer they saw that the cottage was made of food...and the best of cajun *cuisine*. The walls were made of links of *boudin*, the windows were *beignets*, the roof made of *pralines*, the door was covered with *gratons*, and the walk was made of fried crawfish tails. They ate their way to the little house and then started on the house itself.

"Ça c'est bon!" they agreed.

beignets (been yay) fried square dough with powdered sugar
pralines (praw leens) fudge-like candy made with cream, sugar, and pecans.
gratons (grah tons) fried pig skin
Ça c'est bon! (sah say bon) That tastes good!

Suddenly the *zydeco* music stopped and a voice yelled out, *"Cher, pitié! Cher, pitié! Gumbo Filé!* Who nibbles *dans ma maison* today?" The children were so busy eating they didn't see the ugly witch standing beside them. Again she said, *"Cher, pitié! Cher, pitié! Gumbo Filé!* Who nibbles *dans ma maison* today?" The children looked at the witch and then *'T Pousette* bravely said, *"Madame,* perhaps *les enfants* of the very *Jean Lafitte."*

Cher, pitié (sha, pee tay) darling pitiful
Gumbo filé (gum bo fee lay) a sassafras seasoning for gumbo
Dans ma maison (don mah may son) on my house
Les enfants (layz on fon) the children

The old witch opened the door and said, *"Allons, manger, mes petits enfants!"* The children could not resist the smell of *jambalaya* coming from within so they followed the witch inside.

Allons manger (ah lon mon jzhay) Come eat
jambalaya (jom buh lie-uh) A rice dish cooked with meats, herbs, spices and vegetables
mes petits enfants (may pee tees on fon) my little children

The children saw muskrat and nutria skins hanging on the walls and they spotted a large old trunk in the corner of the room with a big gator skin on top. They were led to a table, already set for them. "How 'bout some good *café au lait* and *beignets?*" asked the old woman. *"Oui, merci, madame."* Answered the children.

Café au lait (kaf ay oh lay) coffee milk
Oui, merci, madame (we ma see mah dahm) yes, thank you, madame

As they ate, they began to feel very strange. Then the old witch began to giggle, then laughed aloud, and said, *"Bien bon, mes petits!* You are under my *gris gris* now! *Allons,* you, *petit garçon,* into that crawfish trap! And you *petite fille,* get that broom and start cleaning. After cleaning, we'll start cooking so we can fatten up that *petit frère.* He's just what I need for my *Sauce Patate!"*

Bien bon (bee yehn bon) very good
Mes petits (may pu teet) my little ones
Gris gris (gree gree) magic
Garçon (gah son) boy
Fille (fee) girl
Frère (frair) brother
Sauce patate (saws puh taht) potato stew

And so it went for weeks . . . 'T Poulette cooking, cleaning, and feeding her brother all that *bonne cuisine*. Every week the old witch would open the cage and tell 'T Pousette to stick out his leg to see if he was fat enough. Then the day came when the old witch said, "*C'est le temps!* Start that *Sauce Patate* and tonight we will have a *bon manger!*"

C'est le temps (say ler ton) It's the time
bon manger (bon mon zjay) good eating

After *La Sauce Patate* had cooked all day, the old witch said to 'T Poulette, "*Viens voir ici, petite fille.* Taste this *sauce patate* and tell me if doz seasonings are just right and ready for my special ingredient." "*Mais, non, madame.* I'm a poor trapper's daughter and never tasted such food." replied 'T Poulette. "*Va t'en!* Then I'll do it myself," the old witch said. As soon as she leaned over the pot, 'T Poulette pushed the old witch as hard as she could. The witch fell right into *la sauce patate!* 'T Poulette grabbed the lid and slammed it on the pot. She ran quickly to the crawfish trap and let her brother free.

Viens voir ici (vee yehn wahr ee see) Come over here
Mais, non (mehn, non) Well, no
Va t'en (vah ton) go away

They started running out of the cottage but then remembered the trunk. They ran back to the trunk, threw off the gator skin, and opened the trunk. *Mon dieu!* The trunk was filled with jewels!

Mon dieu! (mon dyur) My goodness!

This was surely *Jean Lafitte's* lost treasure. They stuffed their pockets with jewels and ran into the swamp towards the bayou. When they got to the bayou they recited what they had heard the old witch singing all those weeks: *"Cocodrie, cocodrie,* help me with your *gris gris.* Then jewels you will surely see. *Viens voir ici, viens voir ici!"*

From the dark bayou waters, rose a huge alligator wearing a jewel tiara on his head. The children held out their jewels for him. He signaled them to climb on his back. "Please, *Cocodrie*, take us home, *bien vite!*" begged the children.

bien vite (bee yeh veet) very fast

Old *Cocodrie* swam quickly and before long they were home. Papa was so happy to see them. He told them how Lelia had died from swamp fever and how sorry he was for what she had done. The children told their Papa about the treasure and how *Cocodrie* was waiting to take them back to get it. So they all jumped on *Cocodrie's* back and returned to the little cottage.

After Cocodrie safely brought them home, Papa Vincent decided he would invite a zydeco band to their little village and have a big *fais do do* so he could share his treasure with the whole village. From that day on, the village was known as Port Vincent where *les petits enfants* always ask for their favorite bedtime story of Old *Cocodrie* and the treasure of *Jean Lafitte.*

Fais do do (fay doe doe) a party that goes on late into the night

LA SAUCE PATATE
Compliments of Jack Brignac

1½ lbs. Andouille (or your choice of sausage), sliced
4 medium potatoes, cubed
2 medium onions, diced
2 cloves garlic, finely diced
½ cup of chopped parsley
½ bell pepper, diced
½ cup celery, chopped
3 stalks green onion, chopped
salt, black pepper, and cayenne pepper to taste
4 tablespoons of roux

In a 2- or 3-quart pot, black pot, or thick-bottomed pot, fry the sausage to render the fat. For the roux: Remove the sausage and add 1 cup of flour to the fat and stir until a peanut color. Add onion and 1 cup of water. Cook onion until tender. Add bell pepper and celery. Cook a few more minutes. Add water slowly to make a thick gravy. Add sausage, potatoes, garlic, green onion, parsley, and seasonings to your taste. Simmer for 30 minutes adding water when needed if it becomes too thick. Serve over rice. Ça c'est bon!